D1611262

LOTUS
ELAN

Osprey AutoHistory

LOTUS ELAN

Coupé, convertible; Plus 2

IAN WARD

To the memory of Colin Chapman,
in gratitude for many years of
excitement and pleasure

Published in 1984 by Osprey Publishing Limited
12–14 Long Acre, London WC2E 9LP
Member company of the George Philip Group

Sole distributors for the USA

Osceola, Wisconsin 54020, USA

British Library Cataloguing in Publication Data
Ward. Ian, 1984
   Lotus Elan.—(Osprey autohistory series)
   1. Elan automobile
   I. Title
   629.2′222   TL215.L67
ISBN 0–85045–550–2

Editor Tim Parker
Associate Michael Sedgwick
Photography Mirco Decet

Filmset in Great Britain
Printed in Spain by Grijelmo S.A., Bilbao

Contents

Chapter 1 **An elite parentage** *7*

Chapter 2 **The search for power** *18*

Chapter 3 **Beauty beneath the skin** *36*

Chapter 4 **Refinement for the breed** *60*

Chapter 5 **Abreast of the times** *82*

Chapter 6 **The Elan grows up** *98*

Chapter 7 **Living with a Lotus** *116*

Chapter 8 **Elan revisited** *127*

Specifications *131*

Acknowledgements *133*

Index *134*

CHAPTER ONE

An elite parentage

Despite Lotus's up-market moves in recent years, the Elan, perhaps along with the remarkable Seven, remains the company's most famous road car. Not without reason, either, for it performed at least as well as it looked and amassed serried ranks of drooling admirers who would buy one if only . . . . It survived through four-and-a-half series and their derivatives during an 11-year period and finally succumbed in 1973, mainly because the introduction of Value Added Tax had killed the financial attraction of the kit-built car.

To discover what made the Elan such a success and how it came about, we should first look at Lotus in the years immediately prior to its announcement. The company had entered the club for makers of 'real' cars in 1957, when the type 14 Elite became the first Lotus road car for the ordinary motorist, as opposed to the racing enthusiast. In the style which became so much his trademark, Colin Chapman, founder and driving force of the organisation, had thrown convention out of the window and commissioned a fibreglass monocoque for the new car. The technology of fibreglass was relatively new at the time; although the material did its job admirably in the Elite, the workforce at the factory was not yet skilled in the new science, and so manufacturing standards varied. Apart from the failures which resulted from the enormous stresses imposed by suspension, engine and transmission on

Colin Chapman, founder of Lotus and its driving force until his death at the end of 1982

7

The Elite was Chapman's first practical road car and it defied convention by being constructed around a fibreglass monocoque. It paved the way for the simpler and cheaper Elan

the monocoque, there were problems with inordinately high noise levels. In addition, the six mouldings necessary to make the body/chassis unit were expensive, so it was only a handful of real enthusiasts who could afford to own Elites. The sleek, smooth and elegantly proportioned body from the multi-purpose pen of accountant Peter Kirwan-Taylor was not enough to turn the car into a commercial success, despite a whole series of production modifications.

In the light of this, it was perhaps surprising that the Elite was catalogued for as long as six years. Eventually, Chapman realised that each car sold was actually losing money and the way was open for something simpler. The Elite had brought Lotus to the brink of financial ruin, so some care had to be taken in designing its replacement.

Strangely, the Elan's first stirrings were along lines far removed from its final form. It was intended to be a two-plus-two, still using a fibreglass monocoque, but this time shaped in a single mould to simplify and thus reduce the cost of production. Ron Hickman, who had joined the company from Ford as Design and Development Engineer, was given the task of perfecting the fibreglass technology and then designing a new car to make full use of it. If anything, the problems to be overcome were greater than with the Elite, because the intention was for the two-plus-two to be an open car, thus losing the considerable torsional rigidity imparted to the structure by the roof. Nevertheless, the design team pressed on regardless to work out some means of combining all the master's requirements.

While this was going on, Chapman, impatient as ever, drew up a specification for a backbone chassis in order to try out his ideas for suspension. These were based closely on the Elite layout, continuing

Power for the Elite came from an all-alloy Coventry Climax engine, which, equipped with a single overhead camshaft and twin SU carburettors, produced 75 bhp from its 1216cc

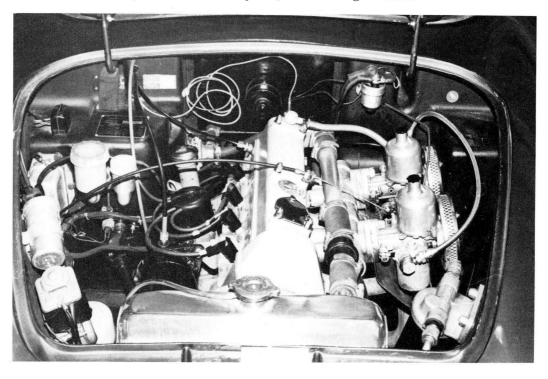

Above *Amid the prosperity of the 1960s, the company had a new factory built at Hethel airfield in Norfolk*

Right *Colin Chapman, with his friend and team leader Jim Clark and a member of the building company (centre), after the chairman had laid the foundation stone for the new plant*

the theme of soft springs and long wheel travel with hard damping to keep a firm check on things over rough and winding roads.

How thankful the designers must have been for this impatience; the makeshift frame turned out to be remarkably stiff, combining a torsional rigidity of more than 4500 lb ft/degree (probably as much as 6000 in production form) with a weight of only 75 lb. This made it about twice as resistant to twisting as the Elite shell, and about six times better than the spaceframe Formula I cars of the period. At a stroke the problems had accidentally been solved: the chassis would happily provide a home for an open-topped fibreglass body, it would be tougher and stiffer than any plastic monocoque and—perhaps most important of all—the whole lot would be much cheaper to produce.

At this point in the story, the brief was still for a two-plus-two, but the theme was steadily adapted until Colin Chapman decided that what the company needed was another two-seater to sell alongside the 'up-market' Elite. This would be a convertible, as already planned, but it would also be a lower-cost and more practical machine than the Elite—less of a road-going racer. The new instruction to the designers was that where the Elite was 60 per cent beautiful and 40 per cent practical, the proportions should be reversed for the open car.

So from around the end of 1961 the planning of this new Lotus proceeded apace, with a fresh set of parameters. The backbone chassis required little work to adapt for production use. It was pressed in sections out of sheet steel and then welded together to form a unit. The secret of its enormous strength lay in the massive central spine, which was a full $10\frac{1}{2}$ in. deep and 6 in. wide, with a bottom panel welded on to complete the box and thus further enhance rigidity. At the front, the frame forked to pass each side of the engine and gearbox, while a

Above *The present factory in Norfolk*

large cross-member linked the forks at the forward end where towers rose to pick up the suspension. At the rear, there was another bifurcation to meet the ends of another cross-member, below which hung the final drive unit. More towers here, together with a rearward extension of the main backbone's bottom plate, provided the necessary suspension mountings. The effect of the whole chassis was of a truncated 'X'.

Although the body would no longer have to provide all the car's structural strength, it was expected to be quite tough in itself, especially as it would furnish the sole support for passengers and luggage and so on would be supported only on the body. It was not made as one moulding, but two. The upper, visible, section, was formed separately from the floor pan and wheel arches, and the two sections bonded together while the fibreglass was curing. None of the fibreglass was impregnated with colour during manufacture. Lotus preferred to spray the car in the normal way, a technique which simplifies accident repair considerably.

Perhaps not surprisingly, there was much more to

Below *October 1962 and the Elan makes its debut at the Earls Court Motor Show, with a price tag, in complete form, of just £1499*

the body shell than a few layers of chopped-strand matting liberally doused in resin. Reinforcement was judiciously incorporated at strategic points—as with everything else Lotus, just enough to do the job without adding a burden of unnecessary weight. A latticework of thick wire struts criss-crossed the door surrounds and the sills—with the effect that the 'official' jacking points could be placed under the latter and be used to raise two wheels off the ground at once. Also, 'paper rope' was built in to the lay-up to stiffen such parts as the bonnet lid. One minor triumph for Ron Hickman was the invention of little aluminium bobbins, which were drilled and tapped, so that when bonded into the fibreglass they could take any mounting bolts needed. In all, 110 of these devices were used around the body and provided really strong anchorages.

The heart of the Elan was its deep backbone chassis, fabricated from pressed-steel to locate the suspension and steering and house engine and transmission

Shortly before the Elan's announcement at the London Motor Show of 1962, only details remained to be sorted out, however. One niggling problem involved the headlights. With a low car such as this, it was always a headache to comply with the British regulation which stipulates that these lights must be at least 2 feet from the ground. The conventional solution usually made the front of a sports car look peculiarly high, and spoilt otherwise sleek aerodynamic lines. The Lotus team had experimented with various arrangements, including Elite style protruding wings, faired-in lamps, *à la* Jaguar E type, and a hinged 'pop-up' system which would both comply with the law and permit the retention of a sloping wing line.

Predictably, it was the last of these which Chapman favoured, and he set to work to perfect an operating mechanism. In an effort to avoid the more obvious—and more failure-prone—electric or hydraulic systems, he opted initially for a manual arrangement, operated from the driver's seat by a lever. However, he was not happy with this somewhat crude set-up and experiments carried out on the M1 motorway with a pair of pop-up lamps mounted on brackets at the front of his Jaguar convinced him that the answer lay in vacuum operation. Small pneumatic motors, metal tanks containing rubber diaphragms, were mounted to swivel the light pods; they were powered from the inlet manifold. A reservoir was required to maintain depression when the throttle was wide open, and the neat solution was to make use of the front chassis cross-member for this purpose. As it turned out, the system worked very well and was remarkably reliable, although leakages in earlier cars caused the lights to drop at high speed.

Considering how quickly the Elan was designed, in perhaps 18 months or two years, compared with four or five years for a modern saloon, it underwent

15

surprisingly few changes between prototype and production stages. We have just seen that various headlamp ideas were tried, but this apart, the only major alteration came in the brake system layout. In the prototype, the rear disc brakes were mounted inboard, next to the final drive, as on the Elite, but whereas the Elite had Hardy-Spicer Hooke-type universal joints, the Elan used rubber couplings, which meant that as soon as the brakes were applied in anger, these would wind up and the car would stop in a series of kangaroo leaps unless the braking pressure was completely even.

Chapman was loath to move the brakes, but neither did he feel able to dispense with the rubber couplings. However, he was forced to compromise and so the brakes were moved outwards, which solved the problem at the expense of increased unsprung weight.

One manufacturing bonus inherent in the use of a separate chassis for the Elan was that all the running gear could be bolted to the frame before the body was fitted on what was by then a rolling chassis. This meant that access was easy, and this in turn sped up the manufacturing process and—most importantly—kept costs down. The extensive employment of proprietary parts, from manufacturers such as Ford and Triumph, helped further in this direction, and when the new car was announced at Earls Court it cost just £1499, complete, compared with more than £2000 for the Elite, which struggled on into 1963, but which was doomed from the moment the much better Elan was revealed. In an effort to increase sales, the factory had made a component form Elite available in October 1961. This meant that purchase tax was not payable, even though very little work was required on the part of the owner to complete the 'kit', and the price could therefore be reduced to £1299. However, the kit theme was continued from the

Elan's inception, so the Elite was still undercut, at £1095. In fact, most Elans started off as component cars, and the factory ran a service whereby the completed vehicles would be given a free check-over and any mistakes rectified. In the case of the Elan, completion of a kit comprised fitting engine, gearbox, exhaust, some front suspension parts, battery and wheels.

So the Elan was born. It received a rapturous welcome from the Press, who acclaimed it with but a single voice as possibly the most effective small sports car of all time. An inspired combination of sleek good looks, light weight, respectable power output and sure-footed nimbleness prompted often cynical journalists to eulogise about the little Lotus in previously unheard of fashion.

It is fitting that the Press presentation of the Elan took place at the London showroom of the Ford Motor Company. As already mentioned, the car used a great deal of proprietary equipment, and by far the most important part of this was the four-cylinder 116E engine which gave Lotus the basis for what has become their very famous 'Twin Cam'.

The headlights were housed in fibreglass pods which, with the aid of engine vacuum, swivelled to move the lamps to and from their operating position

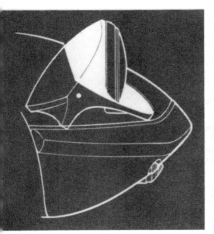
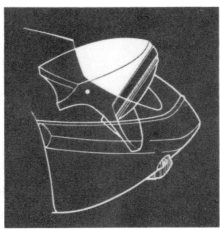
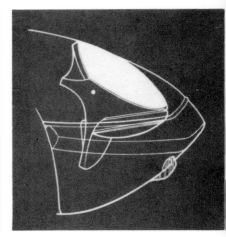

CHAPTER TWO

The search for power

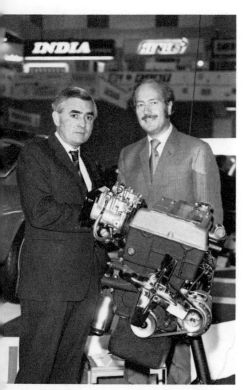

Ford's short-stroke 1500 cc engine provided an ideal basis for the celebrated twin-cam, which powered the Lotus-Cortina as well as the Elan. Here, Chapman and Walter Hayes of Ford mark the power unit's success

Power for the Elite had come from a thoroughbred Coventry Climax engine, the single-cam FWE. This all-alloy 1216 cc unit had been developed especially for Chapman as a combination of the FWA and FWB racing motors—indeed, its name reflected this, standing for *Feather Weight Elite*. It was reliable and efficient, producing 75 bhp in lightly tuned, single-carburettor form, but it was expensive, and its aluminium crankcase transmitted a considerable amount of noise and vibration into the car's shell.

For his new car, Chapman wanted a power unit which would produce a more than adequate amount of power at a much lower cost than that of the FWE; he needed a true production engine rather than one adapted from a racing basis. However, this is not to say that he did not expect the equation to balance the other way round—his new power source should be capable of taking the chequered flag.

All previous Lotus models had been powered by proprietary engines; Coventry Climax apart, these had come from the likes of Ford and BMC. However, although he cast around for a unit to fit the Elan bill, Chapman discovered that there was nothing available 'off the shelf' which would match both cost and performance requirements. He decided that his best course would be to have an engine built especially for the car, and to this end his close association with Ford helped.

The company's executives had let it be known that a five-bearing version of the short-stroke 109E unit would soon be announced. The Lotus boss saw straight away that this would provide an ideal basis for what he wanted; a short stroke meant that the bores were correspondingly large, and this made room for valves big enough to cope with generous gas-flow rates. What is more, the cast-iron four-cylinder block would be much cheaper than the

Most Elan's were purchased in kit form, in order to avoid purchase tax. Constructional tasks left to the owner were few, however, and it did not take much more than a weekend to finish a car

This Series 1, with optional hard top is special because it was the property of Jim Clark, who brought Lotus two world championships before his death in 1968

Climax engine's alloy, and would subdue a considerable amount of the noise and vibration. A sturdy bottom end with ample journal proportions would complete the package, especially when there were five main bearings instead of three—a rarity in mass production power units of the time.

With its 'cooking' pushrod cylinder head, the Ford engine could never provide the kind of sophistication thought desirable for the Lotus, so

A proud owner, complete with carpet slippers, with his Series 1 in 1964

Colin Chapman commissioned Harry Mundy (with assistance from Richard Ansdale) to design a new twin-cam head to fit. The choice of Mundy was no accident, for it was he who, while working for Coventry Climax, had penned the FWA racing engine, the model for the Elite's power source. Having previously also been part of the BRM team, he was at that time—1961—employed as technical editor of *Autocar* magazine, and coincidentally had

21

recently been working on a similar type of head for a stillborn Facel Vega project. Thus, the Lotus design was finalized in a remarkably short time, and soon prototype heads were being tested on over-bored versions of the three-bearing engine.

Tests were successful, with encouraging power outputs from the modified engine proving the worth of Mundy's design. As soon as the five-bearing block became available, the necessary modifications were carried out for mating it to the head.

The head itself was constructed in aluminium alloy, with two valves per cylinder located in hemispherical combustion chambers. Each valve was inclined at 27 degrees to the vertical, and operated through inverted-bucket tappets. Valve clearances were set by means of circular shims of various thicknesses, which could be replaced only if the cams were removed. In my experience the lengthy processes necessitated by this arrangement are extended because the sizes etched in the shims when they are new wear away in use, so that the job cannot be done without a micrometer. Fortunately, however, once set, the clearances tend to remain fixed for a long time. The earliest twin-cams had their tappets running direct in the aluminium, but they tended to 'pick up', so cast-iron sleeves were inserted to solve the problem. Double valve springs made sure that there would be a gas-tight seal at all times when the cams dictated, but unfortunately there were never any valve stem oil seals, and it did not take much wear in this region for an Elan to be followed along the road by a faint blue haze. One or two enterprising engineering concerns with a leaning towards things Lotus have offered seal kits. The real problem, however, lay in the fact that the oil return from head to sump was so constricted that lubricant under pressure built up in the cam box.

The double cams ran in five bearings each, and were turned by a single chain from the nose of the

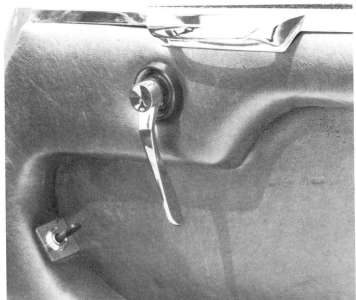

Above *An early Series 2, with glove box and full-width fascia panel, but with S1 door trim*

Left *The S3 had revised door panels hiding its electric window motors and these carried remote door handles. The electric window switch shown here is unusual; most S3s had the switches on the dash*

At one time there were plans to market a child seat for the rear space of the Elan, but these never came to fruition

crankshaft. On its way from bottom to top, this also drove the original Ford camshaft, which was retained to drive the distributor, oil pump and mechanical fuel pump. All three sprockets were standard Dagenham items, with unique Lotus timing marks on the upper pair. A sprung, and externally adjustable tensioner kept the slack side of the chain in order, and a plastic guide reduced noise.

The timing gear was encased in a purpose-built alloy timing cover, into which was set the water pump. The arrangement of this, which once again used mostly Ford components, was such that it had to be assembled into the front cover in bits rather than bolted on as a unit. The system would have

*An unusual view of the
engine bay; the air cleaner
arrangement gives away that
this is a Series 1 car. Straight
from the company sales
brochure of the time*

been fine had the pump been reliable, but its
bearings, and thus its seals, tended to wear, often
because of an over-tight fan belt. Replacement
involved lifting the head and dropping the sump in
order to take off the front cover. I have spent many a
happy hour cursing the umpteen tiny timing cover
bolts, and have been moved to try the short cut of
leaving the sump in place; however, even if the
cover goes back without ruining the sump gasket,
there will usually be a water leak—into the oil—
from around the pump's O-ring seals, so the job has
to be done all over again.

The block itself was standard Ford, at any rate in
the case of the very first units, with a capacity of
1498cc from dimensions of 80.96mm bore and

Elan's were campaigned with great success on the race track, largely due to development carried out by Graham Warner, seen here with his famous LOV 1 at the Goodwood TT of 1963

72.75 mm stroke. However, only a handful of cars were made in this form before the bore was increased to 82.55 to bring the capacity up to 1558 cc. Indeed, it is doubtful whether more than one or two actually found their way into the hands of owners, between the announcement in 1962 and the change in May 1963, since production was very slow to start. Even these were recalled, and their engines changed free of charge.

1558 cc may seem like a whimsical choice of capacity, but there was method in Colin Chapman's madness. Always quick to make the most of racing regulations, he realised that a change in the sports car rules would leave his engine below the maximum permissible size. The new regulations allowed for a maximum capacity of 1600 cc, to be achieved by enlarging the bore of a production unit by no more than 1 mm. Suffice it to say that such an increase on the original 82.55 mm took the twin-cam very close to the limit.

In fact, the Lotus engine had been blooded on the race track in the effective Lotus 23 before the Elan's announcement. In its 1500 form, it had astonished the likes of Ferrari by pushing the 23 to a first-lap lead at the Nürburgring 1000 Km in September 1962. Admittedly, the car benefited from being piloted by Jim Clark, but the engine was in more or less its production form, and was turning out only 100 bhp.

Not every Ford block was capable of accepting the overbore, so special thick-walled ones were picked out for Lotus, and the best ones of all were reserved for racing. The crankshaft was a special Lotus item, although it was still made of cast iron. The con-rods and pistons were similarly unique, the latter having slightly raised crowns with pockets to prevent expensive contact between pistons and valves. In Mark II engines, as

Elans like Graham Warner's were quite capable of taking on and beating the mighty E type Jaguars, even in lightweight trim

Right *New takes on old, as a fastback Shapecraft Elan leads a Team Elite at Silverstone in 1964*

introduced in 1966, these pockets were made slightly smaller, and a few other changes were instigated at the same time. The crankshaft was modified to take a six-bolt flywheel in place of the earlier four-bolt type, and new, tough Ford conrods, marked 125E, were substituted for the original Lotus items. The crankshaft change also brought an improved rear oil seal arrangement, and there were additional subtle MkII developments, such as revised oil pick-up arrangements, which went almost unnoticed.

This last amendment actually did nothing to alleviate the problems of oil surge which prevail in the Elan. I have tried MkI and MkII blocks in my elderly car, and despite efforts to ensure that the oil pick-up pipe is reaching the bottom of the sump, I have always found that unless the level is right up to the 'max' mark on the dipstick the oil pressure will sag to nothing on fast right-hand corners, or under exuberant braking. The only real cure, it seems, is to baffle the sump and keep the lubricant in order.

Below *Elan's were highly competitive at international level. This instantly recognisable S1 is seen at the Nürburgring 1000 Km in 1964*

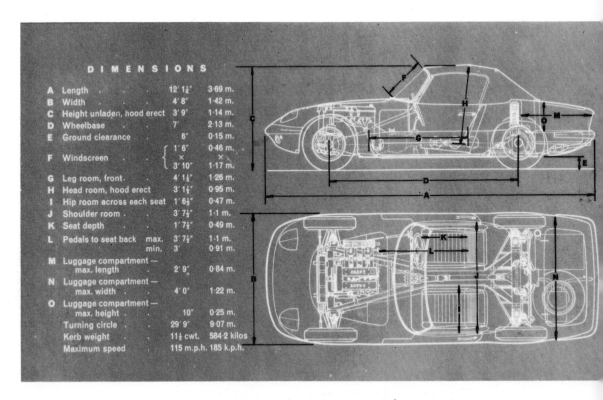

DIMENSIONS

A	Length	12' 1½"	3·69 m.
B	Width	4' 8"	1·42 m.
C	Height unladen, hood erect	3' 9"	1·14 m.
D	Wheelbase	7'	2·13 m.
E	Ground clearance	6"	0·15 m.
F	Windscreen	1' 6"	0·46 m.
		×	×
		3' 10"	1·17 m.
G	Leg room, front	4' 1½"	1·26 m.
H	Head room, hood erect	3' 1½"	0·95 m.
I	Hip room across each seat	1' 6½"	0·47 m.
J	Shoulder room	3' 7½"	1·1 m.
K	Seat depth	1' 7½"	0·49 m.
L	Pedals to seat back max.	3' 7½"	1·1 m.
	min.	3'	0·91 m.
M	Luggage compartment — max. length	2' 9"	0·84 m.
N	Luggage compartment — max. width	4' 0"	1·22 m.
O	Luggage compartment — max. height	10"	0·25 m.
	Turning circle	29' 9"	9·07 m.
	Kerb weight	11½ cwt.	584·2 kilos
	Maximum speed	115 m.p.h.	185 k.p.h.

The Elan measured up

The twin-cam also suffered from an unusual problem with its starting system. The bottom end being largely Ford, the engine was equipped with the standard starter motor, held in place by just two bolts. Now, while this was fine for the low-compression Classic or Cortina, the increased effort required in the Lotus unit caused excessive wear rates in both starter pinion and flywheel ring gear. It seems that the strain was able to bend the starter away from the flywheel enough to cause this, with the result that the starter would either jam almost irretrievably in mesh or simply fail to drive the flywheel round. On many occasions I have experienced both troubles, crawling underneath in my best suit to apply a spanner to the squared starter shaft, or listening with teeth on edge as metal chews metal and the engine turns in fits and starts. The cause of the headache is doubly confirmed by the fact that I have also had to renew a broken starter mounting plate several times; and a specialist company marketed a conversion which enabled a sturdier three-bolt motor to be employed.

An interesting final note on this subject is that the correct pinion for the Ford bottom end had ten teeth, whereas that used by Lotus has only nine. While the overall sizes were the same, the extra tooth, although it unfortunately raised the gearing, brought a more effective mesh. The correct pinion can be obtained through Lucas shops.

Fuel mixture was supplied to the cylinders through a pair of the ubiquitous Weber 40DCOE side-draught carburettors, in effect providing a separate carb for each barrel. An unusual feature was the inlet manifolding, which consisted of four individual stubs cast (and machined) as part of the cylinder head. There was no balance pipe, so it was essential that the Webers were carefully adjusted if tick-over were not to shake the engine off its mountings. Incidentally, the vacuum take-off for headlamp operation—and that of the brake servo when fitted—came from no. 1 cylinder, so any air leaks caused a weakening of the mixture here, and would sometimes lead to valve-burning.

Although these carburettors were standard wear during nearly all of the Elan's life, twin Strombergs were fitted to some Series 4 models, and early Sprints had Dell'Ortos, but more of this anon. A few words of warning for eager owners: do not take a spanner to apparently loose carburettors—they are sealed in place by rubber O-rings and held just tight enough by double-sprung Thackeray washers under the nuts. This flexibility was designed to combat fuel-frothing in the float chambers.

Exhaust systems were changed a few times, but most had a cast-iron manifold to take the gases

Completion of a kit was supposed to be simple enough for women to cope with. Fortunately the feminist movement was yet to be born!

away from the head. The tubular four-branch types were mainly reserved for the Special Equipment and Sprint variants.

Ignition was taken care of by a conventional coil and distributor system; the sparking plugs were fitted into the top of the cylinder head, entering the combustion chambers slightly to one side of the valves. The original distributors had the usual vacuum-advance mechanism, but these were never connected, and it was not long before Lotus dispensed with them on a new distributor type. The rotor arm was a special one, with a centrifugal weight built in to short out the ignition above—in

Checking the alignment of the twin-cam's camshaft bearings

theory—6500rpm, and prevent over-revving. Unfortunately, its operating speed was seldom accurately set, so most owners, this one included, quickly substituted the standard Lucas item.

If ever an engine cried out for electronic ignition, it was the twin-cam. The mechanical set-up worked fine, but the distributor was buried so securely beneath the front carburettor that adjustment of the points required a special short, or angled, screwdriver, a mirror, purpose-built treble-jointed arms and inexhaustible patience. Do away with the contact-breakers, and the problem is solved once and for all.

All twin-cams in their Elan environment had dynamos to generate the electricity—at any rate, all home-market engines did. These were considered adequate for any demand that might be made of the battery, but in fact could not actually keep up if lights, wipers and heater fan were needed all at once. An alternator conversion was simple to carry out, since the necessary parts were available for the Plus 2, but the most annoying generator problem I have encountered has been mechanical rather than electrical. The bracket which fixes the dynamo to the cylinder block is held in place by two large bolts, and these have a habit of releasing themselves, thus depositing the generator on the road, unless they are restrained by a dab of Loctite on their threads. The worst aspect of such a failure is that once freed from its main supports, the dynamo hangs on its upper adjusting strap; this in turn is fixed to the alloy timing cover, and it is this alloy which gives—and necessitates an expensive and time-consuming replacement job.

Harry Mundy's work was well done. For when the Elan was first tried by the Press one of the many compliments paid to it was with regard to the smooth flexibility of its engine. It managed to produce more than a respectable amount of power, but at the same time kept its power and torque bands very usefully wide, despite a high-for-the-era compression ratio of 9.5:1. Perhaps we should let the figures speak for themselves. Original Lotus claims were somewhat optimistic, and for years the standard power output was quoted as 105 bhp at 5500 rpm (100 bhp at 5700 rpm for the 1498 cc original). Later workshop manuals, however, told the truth and gave a figure of 90 bhp, still at the same speed. Perhaps the more important figure was that for torque, which amounted to 108 lb ft at 4000 rpm (102 at 4500 for the smaller unit). Driving an Elan quickly reveals why it was thought necessary to fit an ignition cut-out: the engine gives the impression that it would happily and usefully run ever faster, way past the 6500 rpm red line. It shows no signs of harshness at the top end, and in fact the gearing of many models was such that the Elan would reach maximum of around 115 mph if caution and the rotor arm were thrown to the wind.

Being based on an already extant production cylinder block, the twin-cam was subjected to certain compromises, such as the hidden distributor and the inelegant water pump solution, but it more than compensated in the way it performed.

It was not until Lotus moved to their present home at Hethel that production of the twin-cam finally moved 'in house'. Prototype work was carried out by Cosworth Engineering, who also prepared the early racing units. Then manufacture was put in the hands of J. A. Prestwich, famous for its JAP motors, before that company was absorbed by Villiers, who continued to turn out twin-cams until 1967. After the demise of the Elan, the Plus 2 and the Europa, Caterham Car Sales took over the job, to make engines for the Seven, by now their responsibility. Thus a continuity of supplies was ensured. Lotus, however, eventually reclaimed the tooling, and production finally ceased.

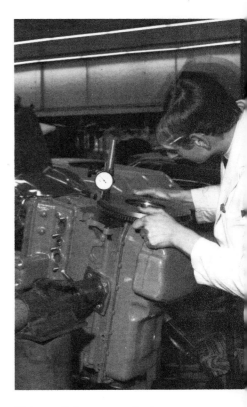

Using a dial gauge to check run-out on the face of the flywheel

Beauty beneath the skin

The heart of the new Lotus was its cleverly adapted backbone chassis. Clothed in the smooth and pretty fibreglass body, which echoed the flowing lines of the Elite without actually copying them, and powered by this effective little engine, the Elan was destined for great things.

A diaphragm spring clutch, suitably uprated from Ford specifications, transmitted the power from the engine to a four-speed, all-synchromesh gearbox. Once again, this hailed from a Ford product, in this case the Classic. It came as standard with what Lotus called semi-close ratios; these were also Ford parts, but special Lotus close ratios were available as an optional extra. The trouble with a small company such as Lotus is that it tends to introduce what are known as running changes. That do not coincide with the announcement of a new model number, and a case in point concerns gearboxes. To the casual eye, there was just one significant change, when the excellent Corsair 2000E box was substituted for the Classic unit. However, other subtle changes were made to ratios and internal construction, which become apparent only when trying to obtain spares. To be fair, much of this headache is due to dear old Henry, with the usual policy of 'continuous improvement', but it does make matters very difficult.

The engine was located in the chassis so that the gearbox was well back under the tunnel. And this meant that there was no need for a remote control gearchange, the short lever going straight into the box, and still managing to be ideally placed for most drivers.

A short propeller shaft joined the box to the chassis-mounted final drive, running through the box section of the central spine. It had universal joints at each end, but these were hardly necessary as its ends were well aligned, and engine or diff

A complete rolling chassis, specially prepared for exhibition, with polished drive shafts etc.

*The fixed-head coupé makes
its debut at Earls Court in
1965 alongside the rolling
chassis shown on the previous
page*

movement came only with torque-reaction or vibration. Any small length changes brought about in the same way were taken up by sliding splines at the gearbox end.

It is the prop-shaft which presented me with one of my most frustrating, infuriating and—in retrospect—amusing repair jobs. A persistent knocking from beneath the car finally revealed itself as the death-knell of a universal joint. I duly went out and bought the requisite repair kit, widely available in motorist's shops, and set about instituting a cure. Off came the shaft—a matter of undoing just four nuts and bolts on the rear drive flange and drawing the shaft out rearwards—on went the new bearing yoke and rollers. Everything was going fine and I'd finish by opening time. . . . First lesson, never plan your day beyond the job in hand if you are venturing into the Lotus unknown. Opening time came and went; so did closing time for that matter. Still I could not coax the prop-shaft back through the tunnel and on to its splines. It was simply not possible to keep the front part of the shaft pointing in anything like the right direction: the forward universal joint kept allowing it to fold down. I tried everything—science, religion, expletive, threat—but it would not go. Then I decided to lift up the carpet which covered the transmission tunnel. There, staring at me, was a large, round rubber bung, next to the tail of the gearbox. I prised this out to find that the hole continued through the chassis to reveal the problem shaft. All I had to do was to slip my by now bruised and bleeding arm in, gently push the shaft on to its splines and replace the bung. It took no more than two minutes to do a job with which I had struggled for hours. Of course if I'd read the manual, or indeed had one at that time, I could have avoided the anguish—but then I'd only have had a hangover!

The final drive itself was a standard Anglia 105E

A rear brake/hub unit, with a torque wrench in use to fasten the brake caliper to the hub casting

item, but to adapt it for use with independent suspension, Lotus built their own aluminium casing, hung from the rear cross-member on rubber Frustacone mountings, and steadied at the bottom by torque-reaction rods running forwards to each side of the chassis bottom panel. The final-drive ratio was 3.9:1; rather low for such a light car, but it endowed the Elan with sparkling acceleration together with a rev-restricted maximum which was more than could often be used on British roads, even before the blanket speed limit.

The arrangement of the drive-shafts was closely linked to Colin Chapman's innovative suspension design. As with any other independent system, the shafts had to be universally jointed—at each end in this case—but they also had to be able to change their effective length with suspension movement. The most common solution to such an automotive poser was to utilize conventional Hooke-type universals together with sliding splines, but Chapman felt that these splines would create unwanted friction and make a nonsense of carefully calculated suspension settings. Thus he plumped for the rubber 'doughnut' Rotoflex couplings to perform both functions. As a matter of interest, his caution had been well placed. In later years, when the Sprint was on the stocks, Tony Rudd experimented with sliding splines, and the handling of the cars became most unpredictable. Apparently, the splines would lock up under torque and thus all but prevent further suspension movement until the torque was removed. The doughnuts were retained—albeit in stiffer form.

More recently, a couple of companies have offered drive-shaft conversions. One retained one Rotoflex, while the other did away with both; it is interesting to note that the latter apparently suffered from exactly the same problem and was heavily criticized. One final important function of the doughnuts is to absorb drive-line shocks and reduce the risk of breakage in any of the components. Of course, all this strain means that the couplings have a limited life, and thus require frequent careful checking for cracks or tears.

The suspension itself followed similar lines to the Elite's, which had what was christened a Chapman strut, a layout which had also been used on Lotus racing cars. The fundamental difference between

Diana Rigg spread the Elan gospel wide when she used a car in television's Avengers *series. Strangely she is seen here with an S2, although it was an S3 that 'Emma Peel' drove*

41

Left *Either a late S1 or an early S2. Running changes meant that this export Elan had S1 door trim with an S2 dash*

Top left *Elan at Elan. A hardtop S2 seen in Wales near its eponymous village*

Above *The rear of a Special Equipment S2, distinguished from S1 and S3 by its clustered rear lights and inset boot lid*

this and the Elan set-up was that the drive shaft on each side formed the lower suspension member in the Elite, whereas there was a large lower A-frame in the Elan to perform this function. The struts were rigidly mounted into alloy uprights at their lower ends, but flexibly mounted by rubber 'Lotocones' at the top. Telescopic dampers were built in, and there were coaxial coil springs. The great width of the A-frames at their inner ends meant that they could provide adequate longitudinal location, so no trailing or semi-trailing links were required. The uprights themselves were substantial, a separate outer shaft running through them and being carried on well separated wheel bearings.

At the front, the suspension was more conventional. Upper and lower pressed-steel wishbones of unequal length connected Triumph Vitesse uprights to the chassis towers, and coil-spring/damper units fed loads to the chassis from the lower one. The wishbones themselves were specially made, and the springs and dampers were unique, but most of the other parts, such as the swivels and trunnions, came from Triumph. The arrangement was completed by an anti-roll bar, running rearwards from the bottom of each spring/damper unit.

Steering, too, was Triumph, with a rack-and-pinion set-up, and a Triumph collapsible column. The only modification to the system was to insert a collar in order to enlarge the turning circle from the taxi-like sweep of the Herald/Vitesse/Spitfire family.

Front disc brakes were another part of the Triumph package, but those at the rear had rarely been seen elsewhere—mainly because so few cars had rear discs. The Elan's had to be special ones to incorporate a handbrake mechanism. In this case, it was a mechanical linkage, with a special pair of pads each side, just for parking. There was no servo on the early cars, and one big nuisance was the fact that the master cylinders for clutch and brakes were buried beneath the carburettors and their large air box. This meant that it was impossible to remove the tops without reaching under the carbs from the front, and very difficult to top the reservoirs up without spilling corrosive brake fluid. Some cars apparently had a form of extension to ease this filling process, but I have never come across one, and space is very tight in that area.

Steel wheels were always the standard apparel of the Elan, lightweight alloy ones being offered only on the Plus 2. On the earliest cars, these were held in place by four bolts, conventional style, but Series 2 versions, introduced in November 1964, were available with a knock-on, centre-lock type, with peg location, as an option: after this time it became rare to see a new Elan with the old-style wheels. Tyre sizes and types changed slightly over the years. When the new Lotus was launched, it came with 5.20 × 13 cross-plies on its $4\frac{1}{2}$ in. rims, but it was not long before the car was given the radials it deserved. Original equipment was the 145–13 size, 155s not even being optional until the introduction of the S4 with its flared wheel arches, but it is very rare today to find any Elan which still sports the narrower rubber. 155–13 tyres, most commonly Dunlop SP Sports which seem to suit the car well, will just fit under the early rear arches, but anything wider will foul the edges.

As we have already seen, most cars had a cast exhaust manifold. This fed into a single downpipe containing a small expansion chamber, about the size of a large fruit tin. At the rear the main silencer ran transversely, the inlet and tail pipes following a tortuous route to connect up to it. S4s and Sprints had a more conventional longitudinal silencer, but of these more anon.

The body sat astride the steel backbone, held in place by 16 bolts of various sizes. One unusual

Right *Between S2 and S3 the door shape was subtly altered, the author's S2 revealing the sharp corner at top right which was rounded off for the next series*

Below *The simple but neat counterbalance mechanism for the non-electric side windows of the S1 and S2*

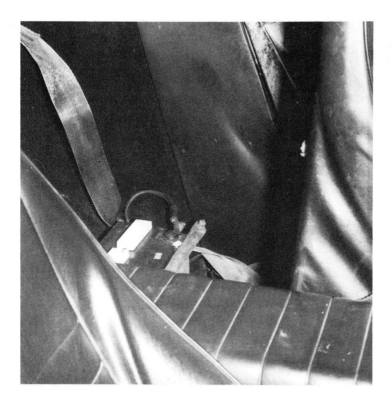

feature about the unit was that it was finished off with fibreglass bumpers at both ends. These may sound rather flimsy, as they would be in their 'raw' state. Lotus, however, filled them with rigid plastic foam, which made them substantial and at the same time provided a resilient backing to absorb minor impacts. In the early days, these could even be ordered with optional chromium plating, to give them the appearance of metal items, but strangely they did not suit the car as well as did the plain silver-painted version.

Another feature which was rare on a small sports car of any type, let alone a limited-production one, was that the doors were of ample dimensions to make entry and exit easy; nothing could be done to help the weak-kneed to overcome the low set of the

The battery was located behind the passenger seat until the advent of the Series 3, which incorporated it into the boot

47

car, but it was simple to manoeuvre the feet in and out because the doors extended well forward into the foot-well areas. The only snag was that there were no keeps to hold the doors open on a slope or in a wind, something which could do the legs no end of harm.

Winding windows were reckoned to add unnecessary complication and take up too much space, so Lotus devised a novel spring-counterbalanced system to control manual sliders. These were frameless, apart from a guide at the front edge, which sealed against the windscreen surround, so when the hood was down the line of the car was completely uncluttered.

The interior door handles acted directly on the catches, which, together with the simple window mechanism, left room for convenient armrests. The high tunnel provided a home for the other elbow.

The two seats were quite basic plastic-trimmed affairs, with fixed backrests, but they provided a good degree of comfort for most drivers and offered plenty of lateral support to cope with high cornering speeds. Fore-and-aft adjustment was generous, and on top of this there were two alternative mounting positions about three inches apart.

To sit in the driving seat was akin to wearing a glove: the door and tunnel fitted snugly round and the steering wheel—originally wooden, but soon vinyl covered—fell readily to hand, as did the gear lever. The pedals were directly ahead, at the end of the deep footwell, which provided almost limitless legroom; they were perfectly spaced for heel-and-toe changes. The only improvement which I have made to my car in this department is to take up some of the safety collapsing travel on the column in order to move the wheel slightly further away.

The high tunnel made the adoption of a lever handbrake impracticable, so an umbrella-handled device was installed beneath the right-hand side of the dash. It was reasonably easy to reach, albeit with the occasional skinned knuckles, as long as you were not wearing the static type of seat belt. It tended to need fairly frequent adjustment in any case, so many owners gave up and left the car in gear when parking. I have watched so many garage mechanics searching in vain, while MoT-testing my car, that I have come to the conclusion that this could be the ultimate anti-theft device!

All the switches were neatly placed and easy to use; two column stalks looked after dipping and indicating. To turn on the headlights, it was necessary first to pull a knob and then to operate the normal light switch—an easy enough operation, but the lights came up flashing even when they were supposedly turned off and most owners modified the wiring to allow the lamps to be kept up and switched off.

Luxury of luxuries, a heater was included in the specification—and a very good one at that. It did not offer the air-blending of today and there were— initially at any rate—no fresh air outlets, but it fed plenty of heat to legs or screen. One of beauties of the deep foot-wells was that they kept the legs out of the draught when the top was down, so the heater was able to continue to do its job.

The early dashboard was an oiled plywood affair, with lidless glove compartment. The instrument display was placed in front of the driver, and comprised speedometer, tachometer, fuel gauge and dual oil pressure/water temperature gauge. Trim was in black vinyl and was quite professional for the type of car, although it was not exactly luxurious. The floors and the rear bulkhead were carpeted, the carpet at the rear wrapping round the battery space behind the passenger seat.

For the size of the Elan, the luggage space was very generous. There may not have been room

Above Series 1 and Series 2 hoods were complex structures with separate four-piece frameworks which had to be removed and stored in the boot if fresh-air motoring was to be enjoyed

Right Perhaps proving that it was practical and reliable as well as fast and nimble, the Elan saw limited service as a police patrol car. This one is an S2 convertible, pictured outside the Cheshunt factory

behind the seats for more people, but you could stow plenty of soft baggage there. Furthermore, the boot could house a big suitcase and some more soft bags, despite the presence of spare wheel and fuel tank beneath its partly wooden-panelled floor. Even the tank was well proportioned, swallowing 10 gallons of five-star.

The first hoods were complicated affairs which did not lend themselves to hasty erection. In my experience, if it does not look as though the rain is going to last long, then press on regardless, because by the time you've dug all the bits and pieces out of the boot and put them together, the sky will have cleared and you will be wet anyway!

*Special Equipment models,
such as this S3, were fitted
with fabricated tubular
exhaust manifolds in place of
the standard cast-iron item*

Because the windows had no frames, the first step in building the top was to slot two fibreglass 'cant rails' into place in an effort to provide some sort of weather seal (of which more follows). Two support bars were then placed between them before the separate hood was fixed on by means of a large number of fasteners. Even then the job was not finished, because the frame needed tensioning from the inside if one was to be sure that the cover would not blow off again.

The early Elans were all convertibles, but the factory did list a separate hard-top—useful in winter, although you had to find somewhere to keep it when it was not needed, and this meant that there was a strong temptation never to remove it.

So that was the Elan as it stood at its launch in 1962. In the Lotus classification system, it was numbered 26—and by way of digression it is interesting to note that it follows the legendary type 25 Grand Prix car which brought Jim Clark and Lotus their first World Championship. The significance of this is that the Elan's backbone supposedly formed the basis for the monocoque which made the 25 so superior to anything before it. Colin Chapman reasoned that for a single-seater, all you needed to do was to split the backbone into two and move the halves apart until you could fit the driver between them. This may be an oversimplification, but there is no doubting the effectiveness of the idea, which moved the spaceframe into history overnight.

There was some delay in getting the Elan into full production, but by May 1963 it was really on the market. It was soon evident that the original projected supply rate of ten cars a week would be totally inadequate. The success of the new car was such that forty Elans, mostly in component form, were soon leaving the Chesthunt, Hertfordshire, works each week. After the move to Norfolk, the figure rose to sixty.

SEs and Sprint models sported brake servos, located ahead of the radiator

The front of the author's S2 was reduced to this pile of scrap by a blind Frenchman and a new half-front was required to put matters to rights

Virgin fibreglass, waiting to be installed

Road testers were almost ecstatic in their praise. Some were in danger of exhausting their supply of superlatives, when it came to describing the near-perfect combination of high power-to-weight ratio and agile, thoroughly predictable handling. For the record, the car was 12 ft $1\frac{1}{4}$ in. long, and 4 ft 8 in. wide, had a wheelbase of 7 ft, front and rear tracks (originally) of 3 ft 11 in., and weighed just $11\frac{1}{2}$ cwt. With these dimensions and a steering ratio giving $2\frac{1}{2}$ turns of the wheel from lock to lock, it becomes more obvious why the Elan was so nimble.

Inevitably, however, there was room for improvement. Thus November 1964 saw the announcement of the Series 2 model, which was substantially the same car, but featured a number of subtle improvements. The most obvious distinguishing feature was the new rear lamp design. Those of the S1 had been individual units, indicators and stop/tail lights, while the second series incorporated these into clusters borrowed from Vauxhall. Knock-on wheels graced most S2s, and a new flip-up filler cap gave a further clue. Inside, the oiled dash was replaced by a varnished one, with a slightly revised switch layout and a proper lockable glove box (later S1s had been blessed with a lid for the cubby hole, but it was still crude). On the inside of the doors, the handles and trim were altered, and smaller pedals completed the interior changes. Beneath the surface, the front brake calipers were enlarged to improve the already excellent stopping power.

It is with an S2 that I had my first Elan encounter. Mine was quite a late example, having first been registered in October 1965. In the time that I've owned it, I have come to know just about every nut and bolt which holds it together. Most things that could go wrong, have, but—touch wood—it has never actually left me stranded, apart from a time when a mad Frenchman U-turned so close in front that it was beyond even the Lotus's powerful brakes to stop. I've cursed and I've sworn at it, but my enthusiasm for it has never faltered.

Even today, when more modern, sophisticated, and certainly more expensive, equipment should have put it well and truly in the shade, it still sets standards by which to judge the rest. My work as a journalist allows me to sample most new cars when they are announced; many of them are excellent in their way, and the majority are more refined, but hardly any show either the capabilities or the sheer character of the Lotus.

The engine pulls the little car savagely away from the line if pressed, and yet will chug along in docile fashion at 25mph in top gear, if asked to do so. The splendid driving position wraps the car round the driver so that he can feel what it is doing at every moment, and the superbly neutral handling combines with delicate and positive steering to give rail-like cornering even at the highest speeds. The tyres simply go on hanging on, even in the wet, and the most callous abuse of the throttle under such circumstances fails to make the car flinch. Most amazing is how Chapman managed to achieve this fly-like ability to change direction at the same time as providing a relatively comfortable ride; it may not be in the luxury limousine class, but it does not jar the spine, as does much of the so-called competition.

Cold performance figures do not really begin to show what a good Elan is like to drive, but they do give a clue to the overall efficiency of the package. Contemporary road tests recorded 0–60mph times in the region of 9 seconds and a maximum of around 115mph; what is more, they found, as I have done, that no matter how hard you try it is all but impossible to drag the fuel consumption below 25mpg.

The Elan, especially the soft-top, is not the

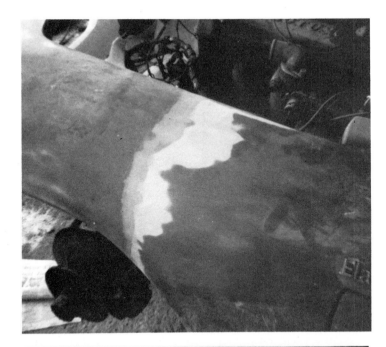

The new half-front was bonded to the old material with resin and matting and the joint finished with a skim of filler

The finished job—successful but hard work

quietest of machines, but the noise from the engine stirs rather than annoys, and it encourages large amounts of floor-bending around the accelerator pedal with spirited use of the gearbox. Even wind roar is not too tiresome; the frameless windows tend to be sucked away from the cant rails at speed, when the hood is in place, but at other times progress is quite refined.

When it's raining, it is a different story. Although the hood of cars like mine actually prevents the water from dropping straight in on your head, the battle has only just begun at that point. The door-sealing arrangements were somewhat primitive and ineffective in these models, failing to provide a continuous water barrier. Thus air pressure forces the wetness in, and once through the door it contrives to run along the lower edge of the dash and drip persistently on to your unsuspecting legs.

It was during the currency of the Series 2, in January 1966, that Lotus announced an alternative Special Equipment or S/E edition. Here was a car with even larger helpings of typical Elan delights. New camshafts and rejetted carburettors raised the power output, supposedly to 115 bhp at 6000 rpm. However, in truth the gain was just 3 bhp, the new peak figure being 93 bhp. Torque remained the same as before, but the small power gain teamed up with a higher, 3.55:1, final-drive ratio and the now-standard close-ratio box to produce a significant performance boost. With the cut-out removed, road testers managed to whisk the little bullet up to nearly 125 mph, and the 0–60 mph time fell to under 8 seconds.

Lotus sensibly left the suspension set-up of the Elan alone, but they did add a servo to improve the already excellent braking. In fact, it is debatable as to just how much of an improvement this represented. Certainly the car would stop quicker for a given pedal pressure, but ultimate braking ability was just the same, and the pedal no longer communicated so clearly what the brakes were doing. I have tried servo-assisted Elans on many occasions, and I am convinced that the best move if you have an S/E is to thow away the servo and fit the softer standard pads.

Other S/E modifications were minor. Special badges identified the model, as did the centre-lock wheels and side flasher repeaters.

The final version of the type 26 Elan—and I use the full title advisedly—was the lightweight 26R, built for competition purposes. Put together by Lotus Components Ltd, the 26R was considerably more expensive than its roadgoing sister, costing £2450 in 1966, compared with just over £1600, including purchase tax, for the contemporary production model. It was also a very different animal.

Weight was saved by using thinner fibreglass for the body and magnesium for the wheels, rear suspension uprights and final drive casing, while some stiffening was added to the chassis. Further savings were achieved by throwing away the heavy bell housing, tailshaft housing and radiator and substituting aluminium items. The suspension itself was stiffened, lowered, and made adjustable by means of Rose joints, while the Rotoflex couplings gave way to metal ones, with roller splines to cope with length changes. Improved brake-balance came with smaller rear discs and twin master cylinders, and a limited-slip differential kept the power going down on the tightest turns.

The engine was breathed on by the likes of Cosworth or BRM to turn out at least 140 bhp (many produced considerably more), and with this specification the 26R provided a basis for some very successful racing machines.

Refinement for the breed

The most important set of modifications to the Elan came in the shape of the Series 3; in fact these were considered major enough by the factory for the 26 type number to be dropped. As usual, the changeover was not a simple one, for it was in September 1965, in the middle of the S2's life, that the first S3 examples appeared. At the time, they were not so titled, because the most noticeable thing about the new cars was simply that they had fixed roofs. Thus, although their type number was 36, they were identified only as Elan fixed-head coupés, which belied the several less obvious body modifications to have taken place.

Unlike the earlier detachable hardtop, the roof of the fixed head coupé could not be removed, even if the sun shone. However, if anything it made the already silky smooth lines of the car even sleeker, and enhanced the neatness of the interior no end. Only the reversed slope of the side windows' rear edges gave an external clue to the more significant improvements within. The change to electrically wound glasses certainly increased the appeal of the Elan, in terms of gadgetry, but the drive arrangements were somewhat Heath Robinsonian, and lacked the ruggedness of the manual arrangement. The converted wiper motors shifted the windows at a snail's pace, and the thin wires which connected spindles to glass were prone to snapping or slipping. The sight of my brother struggling to make fingers fit where they're not meant to in order to refit a recalcitrant cable to his S3 has made me thankful for my old-fashioned S2!

No, this was not a leap forward in itself, but the doors had sprouted frames for those windows now, which meant that the glasses would no longer billow in the breeze to let in an icy draught. What is more, the doors themselves were slightly reshaped, and the sealing system completely altered in a

Colin Chapman posing in 1965 alongside a plaque celebrating a second world championship and an example of the new fixed-head coupé. Note the chrome-plated bumpers, which were optional for a time

Left *The 1000th Elan, an S3 fixed-head coupé, changes hands in 1965. More than 12,000 examples of the two-seater were eventually built*

Above *This is a Special Equipment version of the Series 3 fixedhead coupé, as confirmed by its side-repeater flashers as well as its badge. The ventilation grilles in the rear pillars identify the car as a late model S3*

A convertible Series 3 with its hood in place. Erection of this was much easier than on the S2, as the whole assembly folded into a tray behind the passenger compartment

pretty successful attempt to keep the weather out once and for all. At least now there would be some point in having carpets other than to act as sponges to soak up the contents of the aptly named foot-wells!

Inside, forward-mounted remote handles were added to open the doors, and new, smarter trim panels had smaller armrests. The dashboard was altered a little to feature plastic trim along its lower

Left *The first Elan model, the S1, is hard to find in 1983. Not many were made and everyone knows how Lotuses can fade away somehow. Classic, simple shape – but so effective*

Below *The S1 featured the two separate rear lamps either side of the registration plate – the easiest way to tell an S1 quickly. Note the 'Lotus Elan 1600' badge on the tail also*

Top left *Author Ian Ward's S2 of 1965 vintage. The pretty knock-on disc wheels certainly add style to this convertible. Regular maintenance helps to keep them alive. Note the change in tail lamps and the lack of side window frames*

Bottom left *An S3 of 1966. Lotus Cars managed successfully to blend the design of the hood with the overall shape of the car. Something many other sports car manufacturers constantly failed to do. Note the S3's window frames*

Above *Stark cockpit for this 1969 Elan Special Equipment. You got mostly what you needed but not much more. Few drivers cared, though*

Above *This Elan S4 Sprint certainly looks in good shape. The bulge in the bonnet line is obvious here – designed in to clear the Stromberg carburettors fitted. Note also the chrome wheel trims and the new Europa-style rear lamps*

Top right *1972 Lotus Elan Sprint – two tone paint and divided side strip with the words on the door. This Elan never lacked power!*

Bottom right *An open Elan Sprint with non-standard wheels and the wrong signature on the driver's door. A superb car, nevertheless. This one was one of the very last 1973 cars before production ceased*

Left *Any Elan is pretty in a mid to dark hue. Red seems to suit them particularly well. This same 1969 Elan SE seems up together, the gold bumper adding to that effect*

Above *Unusual to see an 'average' Elan being used everyday on the street in the United States. This one was shot in Rapid City, South Dakota having parked all night with its headlamps still popped up. It may be tired but it's still running*

Above and right *The Lotus Elan Plus 2 brought a certain amount of sophistication to the Elan series even if it's difficult to pin down exactly why, for the technical specification was very similar. Note the two-tone paint and knock-on cast wheels*

edges, and the switchgear layout was revised. The S3's battery was moved from its unorthodox but unobtrusive position inside the cockpit to the boot, where it took up useful stowage space in the nearside rear wing.

A further bodily improvement came in the region of the boot. The early cars had a flat lid which fitted into a hole in the deck. This worked well enough, but the only way that water could run away from

Another SE Series 3, showing how the door frames remained in place when the hood was folded and stowed under a neat tonneau cover

Two versions of the S3 from 1966, both S/Es. Major alterations from the S2 were the framed electric windows and a boot lid which incorporated the rear edge of the body

the channel round it was through tubes moulded
into the fibreglass at the rear, which fed to the
outside world through the lower part of the bumper.
Unfortunately, these became blocked rather quickly and rain would soon find its way into the luggage
compartment through seals that were less than 100
per cent effective. I have always made sure that I
poke out these drain tubes regularly, using the
flexible outer part of an old throttle cable for the
purpose, but no matter what I do they seem to

*An S3 somewhat off the
beaten track. This is probably
a prototype, in that the Series
3 convertible was not officially
introduced until June 1966
and this car has a 1965
registration plate*

conspire against my efforts. This headache was removed from the S3 onwards by extending the boot cover backwards to wrap over the rear body edge. Not only was this lid stiffer, so that it sealed better, but the rain could run away without the need for special facilities.

Bolt-on wheels had by this time disappeared. For a long time, incidentally, the radial tyres were fitted with tubes, on the basis that the cornering potential of the Elan was so high that tubeless rubber might

Although this is a 1966 picture, the fixed-head coupé S3 in the background still sports bolt-on wheels, which were hardly ever specified by then. The enlarged and stiffened boot lid of the S3 solved the water leakage problem of earlier Elans

Right *The Series 3 hood arrangement exposed. The framework folded up out of a well behind the passenger compartment and clipped to the screen, the cover then fastening at front and sides*

Below *A well worn Series 3 engine, complete with patched top hose and almost paint-free cam cover*

slip on the rims and deflate. Presumably this never actually happened, because the tubes were quietly dropped.

Other S3 changes were minor. There were new exterior door handles, a Triumph Spitfire radiator in place of the larger purpose-built original, and a modification of which few seem aware, a slightly revised windscreen shape—identifiable principally by its square lower corners.

The S3 fixed-head coupé and the S2 convertible were produced concurrently for six months until the Series 3 drop-head finally appeared, with the number 45, in June 1966. Made mostly on the same moulds as the fixed head model, the new car incorporated all that machine's improvements, and added a vastly better hood to the package. Gone was the separate kit of parts to keep the weather at bay. This top was permanently fixed at the rear and folded up, frame and all, from a recessed tray behind the cockpit to clip on to the screen. A half-tonneau kept things ship-shape when the hood was folded away. If there was a drawback with the new convertible, it was that the permanently positioned window frames cluttered the line of the Elan when the top was off, but this was a small price to pay for sophistication.

Mechanically, the S3 was little changed. The 3.55:1 final drive was an optional extra, and later cars sported a new 3.77:1 ratio as standard, which raised the top speed without an undue adverse effect on acceleration. An incessant chatter from the gear lever was cured after some time by installing a Metalastic bush in the base of the lever itself, although unfortunately this had the side effect of making the change a little rubbery.

I have been fortunate enough to drive all models of Elan and I have found that it is between the Series 2 and 3 cars that the difference is most immediately noticeable from the driving seat. The

Above and top far right *It was Lotus policy to commemorate its racing successes by means of appropriate badging in its production cars*

Sprint may be faster, but the S3 represented more of a leap forward than the Sprint's step. The reason is that the body changes made the S3 an altogether more solid car, free of—or at least less weighed down by—the rattles that could bedevil the previous types. The doors would close with a solid 'clunk', and the improved integrity of their seals

would make the cockpit somehow more cosy. In S/E form, the Series 3 could go like the wind and yet leave its driver completely fresh at the end of a long journey.

But more was yet to come . . . .

Left The Elan instrument arrangement remained unchanged throughout the car's life, but the dashboard style altered slightly (this S3 having crash padding on its lower edge) and the switch type and layout varied from model to model

Abreast of the times

The Series 3 remained little changed throughout its production life, which spanned two years, but by 1968 Chapman felt that the design could do with freshening up once more in order to keep up with modern trends. Thus, March of that year brought the announcement of the Series 4 Elan, still very much the same car—and continuing the type number lines—but subtly altered once more, both within and without.

Most obvious was a flaring of the wheel arches, front and rear, to make way for the wider, 155-section, tyres which were at first optional on S/E versions and later standard on all. In fact, the body was actually stiffened at the same time, a move which meant that late editions were less prone to the surface crazing which had bedevilled previous models. New, bold, rear light clusters, borrowed from the Europa, replaced the Vauxhall units, and the flasher repeaters and chrome wheel-trims of the previous S/E models became fixtures.

A bulge on the right-hand side of the bonnet lid gave a clue to changes in the engine bay. Which actually revolved around the fitting of a pair of Stromberg 175CD carburettors in place of the traditional Weber 40DCOEs. Emission regulations had forced Lotus to equip the cars thus for the American market, with complex pipework to make use of exhaust heat, and it was found that these units, with the emission equipment removed, could match the power developed with the Weber installation. The cylinder head casting was altered to a two-port design to facilitate their adoption, and new camshafts helped to keep the power up. As a matter of fact, the first S4s did still have Webers, the Strombergs not coming in until November 1968, and it was less than a year before the Webers were back in favour, although Stromberg heads went on being used up into 1970. Other engine changes included a

The fourth series of Elan brought more refinement in 1968. The most obvious change was flaring of the wheel arches to give adequate clearance for the 155 × 13 tyres and the adoption of new rear light clusters

Right *The bonnet bulge of this 1969 example covers Stromberg carburettors*

Below *The Stromberg CD carburettors were originally installed in order to meet US emission requirements, but were adopted for British S4s for a year or so. Siamezed inlet stubs distinguished the Stromberg-type cylinder head*

The S4s Triumph-derived radiator was smaller than the S3's similarly originated unit, which itself was less capacious than the purpose-built item of the S1 and S2. An electric fan replaced the engine-driven unit

Right *The S4 tonneau cover had a piece which could be removed separately for driver access*

Below *New rear light clusters for the S4 were borrowed from the Europa and Plus 2 and incorporated reversing lamps*

Above *This view of an Elan
highlights its smooth flowing
lines, although the headlights
of this particular example
require adjustment. The
windscreen wipers, parked on
the left, appear to come from
an export model*

revised cast-iron manifold (tubular for S/Es), which fed a new exhaust system, incorporating a central, longitudinal silencer or siamezed pair of silencers. Yet another smaller radiator was cooled by a new, thermostatically controlled, electric fan and the headlight operating mechanism was reversed, so that in the event of vacuum failure the lights would rise rather than fall (the presence of this 'failsafe' arrangement is betrayed by the lamps slowly rising when the car is parked).

The fuel tank's capacity was reduced to $9\frac{1}{4}$ gallons in order to make room for the enlarged spare tyre. Although most Elan's are now equipped with the 155 tyres, it is necessary to let the spare down in order to fit it beneath the boot floor—if it has more than a minimal tread on it.

Right The S4's fuel tank capacity was reduced to $9\frac{1}{4}$ gallons from the earlier 10, in order to accommodate the larger spare tyre in the boot

Opposite The S4 and Sprint dashboard is instantly recognisable from its rocker switches and fresh air vents. Flush door handles were a further change from the S3

Jochen Rindt, who posthumously became World Champion in 1970, posing with a Sprint prototype. Note the non-standard colour scheme

Above *A non-standard
steering wheel graces this
Sprint, which also features a
steering lock/ignition switch
in place of the earlier
straightforward keyswitch*

Left *Bright metal trims give a
smart appearance to the
wheels of this 1972 Sprint.
US specification centre-lock
nuts have been used in place
of the normal three-eared type*

*Jochen Rindt's 1970
championship is recognized in
the badging on this 1972 car*

Once again the interior was modernized. Flush-fitting Morris Marina handles were set into new-style door trims, in ventilated plastic to match the revised seat coverings. On the dash, fresh air vents, small but nonetheless effective, had sprouted at each end, and the old toggle switches had been replaced by modern rockers. At some time during the S4's currency the traditional key start was ousted by a steering lock, which for the first time gave the convertible cars some measure of security against theft.

Behind the wheel, the standard S4 felt much the same as its immediate forebear, but a sort of Series 4 MkII appeared in February 1971 to change all that. This was the Elan Sprint, last and undoubtedly best of the line. Updating on the Sprint was probably less than most people think; it was very much a higher-performance variant of the S4, identified principally—on the first cars at any rate—by a distinctive two-tone colour scheme with the legend 'Elan Sprint' emblazoned on the dividing stripe.

The engine had been breathed upon by Tony Rudd to produce a genuine 126 bhp at 6500 rpm, with 113 lb ft of torque at 5500 rpm. The lion's share of the increase came from enlarging the inlet valves—as witnessed by the words 'Big Valve' writ large on the cam covers—and raising the compression ratio to 10.3:1. The Stromberg camshafts were retained and Dell'Orto carburettors installed as a temporary measure until suitable settings were achieved for the Webers. A fabricated tubular exhaust manifold became standard and the longitudinal silencer was retained.

At the rear, the chassis was braced to withstand better the additional torque of the big-valve engine, and the Rotoflex couplings were beefed up for the same reason. It was said that the stiffer doughnuts spoilt the ride of the Sprint, but I regard this as a

Only the badges and the colour scheme superficially distinguish the Sprint from the S4

Some Sprints had a single silencer like this, while others sported two siamezed units

perfectly plausible theory completely disproved by practice. No sensible Elan owner today would fit the Hillman Imp-type couplings, which have so short a life, and having used the Sprint variety for years I am convinced that there is no measurable deterioration in ride or handling.

With the extra power, one might have expected the 3.55 final drive to become standard wear, but as the Sprint title implies this car was built to streak away from the line and cruise happily at Britain's legal limit of 70mph; maximum speed was academic.

Even so, the latest Elan would manage around 120mph, which could be improved upon considerably with the installation of the higher axle ratio. Acceleration, as intended, was electrifying for such a small-engined machine—60mph came up from a standstill in less than 7 seconds, leaving drivers of other supposedly quick machinery open-mouthed.

The Elan had never lacked power, but to drive a Sprint was to realise just what you'd been missing. The thrust in the back was sensational, and the

The heart of the Sprint was the big-valve version of the ubiquitous twin-cam, which produced 126 bhp and gave electrifying performance

This manufacturer's plate identifies the car as a type 36—a fixed head coupé, and the unit number tells that it is a Sprint

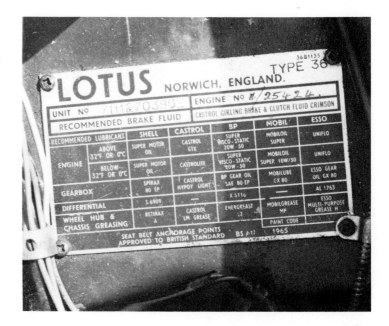

little rocket would be past even quite fast-moving traffic in the blink of an eye. It was only when cruising at really high—and illegal—speeds that the gearing became a nuisance. The drone of the engine was far from irritating, but its obvious reserves of power made the search for a fifth gear a frequent diversion.

As it happens, the last few Elans were equipped with a five-speed gearbox, better known for its use in the late-model Plus 2s. This, in fact was very similar to the unit used nowadays in the front-engined Lotus models, and was perhaps being tested for greater things at the time. Thus equipped, the two-seater would have been capable of around 130 mph, without losing any of its zest.

Sadly, the Elan was dropped from production in August 1973, before enough five-speed models escaped. Some 12,200 had been made over a period of eleven years, and the closing of the line hailed a very definite end to a great era.

For a time Dell'Orto carburettors ousted the famous Webers such as these on the Sprint, but the traditional units were soon back

The Elan grows up

As we saw earlier on, the Elan was first mooted as a two-plus-two Elite, but it was not until 1963 that the idea next raised its head. Even then, it was four more long years and many painful prototype stages before the Elan Plus 2 finally saw the light of day in June 1967. The first prototype, known as the Metier, was smaller in every dimension than the finished item, type 50, which was very much an enlarged version of the two-seater, with instantly recognizable styling. The Plus 2 was 23 in. longer, 10 in. wider and 1 in. higher than the original, with its wheelbase stretched by a foot and its track by 7 in. Unlike the two-seater, it only ever came from the factory in fixed-head form, although some examples were converted by specialists—and very stylish they looked, too. The sleekness of the fibreglass body, which some observers considered to be an improvement over the Elan's, was confirmed by a drag coefficient of 0.3, compared with 0.32 for the two-seater.

Like its smaller brother, the Plus 2 was available in component form, thus escaping purchase tax, and as such it cost £1672. Fully built, the price went up to £1923 inclusive.

The backbone frame was simply an elongated version of the smaller car's, and it carried an identical suspension layout, with altered spring/damper rates to cope with an extra 3 cwt of *avoirdupois*, and longer wishbones, A-frames and drive-shafts to increase the track. Steering, too, used the same parts, but again the linkages were lengthened. Larger front discs, from the Triumph GT6, altered brake balance, and a servo was fitted from the start. The body was made in similar fashion to the two-seater's, but steel stiffeners were moulded into the door sills to replace strength lost by the stretched wheelbase. Steel front and rear bumpers, from Ford Anglia and Wolseley Hornet respec-

An early prototype model, betraying a family resemblance to the production Plus 2

Right The same prototype, with an estate back added

Below Much more like the real thing, this prototype displays the name 'Elite 2'

*A Plus 2 goes through the
spray booth at Hethel*

Elan Plus 2 and Europa body shells together in the Hethel works

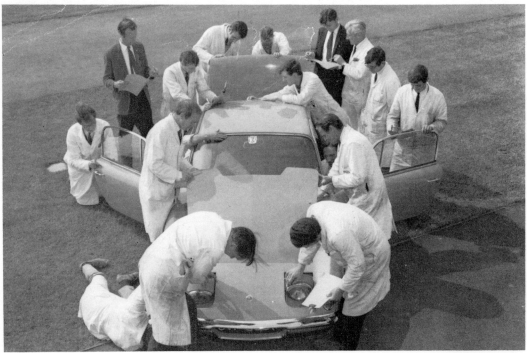

tively, ousted the Elan's plastic items, but the pop-up headlight arrangement was retained, although the lamps were mounted inboard of the wings in the front panel, where they looked somewhat inelegant when in use.

The good old twin-cam engine was installed, but it was never used in standard tune for the Plus 2. In fact three more bhp were coaxed out of the S/E unit in this application, to give a claimed 118bhp at 6250rpm—although the actual DIN figure was more like 95bhp. The S4's Stromberg carburettors never found their way on to British Plus 2s, and the early versions had their own cast iron exhaust manifold, together with the usual transverse silencer. As with the two-seater, a fabricated manifold later became standard, coupled with a longitudinal silencer, which was installed when the luggage boot was enlarged—partly by this means, partly by standing the spare wheel on its edge. The fuel tank capacity was reduced at an early stage from 15 to 13 gallons.

Above There is no mistaking the heritage of the Plus 2— very much an enlarged version of the two-seater

Top left One of the earliest Plus 2s, a 1967 example

Bottom left A Plus 2 undergoes a thorough final inspection under the factory's Quality and Reliability scheme

A set of Plus 2S models, with
a Plus 2S 130 on the right

The forward part of the rolling chassis from a Plus 2S 130, showing the big-valve engine nestling in the fork of the pressed-steel frame

The usual Ford gearbox was employed, with the same internal ratios, but the 3.77:1 final-drive ratio was adopted from the start. The knock-on wheels had the same centres as those of the smaller machine, but 5½ in. rims were substituted and shod with 165-section radial tyres.

The major differences came inside the Plus 2. It was still a two-door car, but the doors were wider and thicker, more luxurious seats tilted to offer

access to the rear (in fact all Elan seats tilted, but generally to no real purpose). The rear seats were designed for children and they were too small, with far too little legroom, for an adult to ride far without acute discomfort. The backrests were very upright, and width was restricted by the chassis widening out at that point.

Electric side windows were installed from the beginning, with remote interior door handles and a

The Plus 2 front and rear suspension links and drive shafts were longer than those of the two-seater. A further difference lay in the incorporation of a heat shield above the rear disc brakes, as seen here

*Elan Sprint and Plus 2S
models share the Lotus motor
show stand with a Europa
Twin-Cam in 1971*

The Plus 2S 130 is easily distinguished from its predecessors by its silver roof. Under the bonnet it hid the 126 bhp big-valve engine

decent standard of interior trim. The extra width meant that the door recesses with armrests were unnecessary, but this was not an improvement. The padded tunnel cover was carried over, and even contained a tiny map locker. The smart dashboard, with built-in glove compartment, was finished in highly polished walnut veneer and had large fresh air vents at each end. Instrumentation was more comprehensive, with the addition of an ammeter and the separation of oil pressure and water temperature gauges. The minor controls were improved, particularly those for the heater, but the umbrella handbrake remained.

As with the basic Elan, contemporary road tests were generous in their praise of the Plus 2. Most found it a far more refined machine than its two-seater counterpart, with enhanced ride qualities and lower noise levels. More than this, though, the greater wheelbase and track dimensions made the Plus 2 even surer-footed than its stablemate, handling in much the same neutral way, but hanging on at even higher cornering speeds. Criticisms mainly concerned the car's straight line abilities. It was quite quick enough for most, with a 0–60 mph time of around 9 seconds and a maximum speed of 120 mph, but many testers asked why the 3.55 axle had not been used, or suggested that a fifth gear would provide a marked improvement.

Prayers were eventually to be answered in this direction, but the first real change to bless the Plus 2 was the announcement of the Plus 2S in October 1968. Mechanically identical to the older model, the S had a more lavish specification, and was put on sale alongside the cheaper version. As it transpired, a production S did not actually leave the factory until March 1969, and the Plus 2 was dropped in December, so they were actually only simultaneously available for a few months. One indication of the way that Chapman intended to take Lotus in years to come was that the Plus 2S could be bought only as a complete car. This meant that the company was hoping to sell its cars to a new, more wealthy and more sophisticated type of buyer.

Nearly all the alterations were inside the cockpit. The ammeter was exchanged for a voltmeter, an outside-temperature gauge and clock were added to the display, rocker switches replaced the earlier toggles, and flush door handles were fitted. Lights appeared all over the place: there were a map light, a glove locker light, lights in *all three* ashtrays, red door warning lights, fog lights, a boot light and even an underbonnet light. Perhaps it was just as well that the dynamo was ousted by an alternator a year or so later.

Although more refined, the Plus 2S was the same to drive as the basic version. February 1971, however, brought the Elan Sprint big-valve engine, with its 126 bhp, to the bigger car, still with the irritatingly low axle ratio and with the stiffer Rotoflex couplings. Designated the Plus 2S 130 (the latter number supposedly representing maximum speed), the revised car could quickly be identified from its silver roof—self-coloured, while the rest of the body was sprayed. Performance was almost as spectacular as that of the Sprint; maximum speed was hardly altered, but the new Plus 2 could rush to 60 mph in a little over 7 seconds—and it could still manage a consumption of around 25 mpg, despite the low gearing.

It was right at the end of the Plus 2's life that the fifth gear finally came, as an option, to give the car the even more cumbersome title of Plus 2S 130/5. Fourth gear was still direct, so that top gave relaxed cruising, rather than an ultimate performance boost. Most tests of the time demonstrated that both acceleration figures and top speeds were as before, but, although the box required some development (which it has since had in the Elite/Eclat range), journalists were agreed that this was a tremendous leap forward.

The Plus 2 was not suddenly and decisively withdrawn from production, as the two-seater had been. Indeed, it continued for more than a year after the last Sprint had left the works. However, by this time, the new, up-market models were needing more space and the Plus 2 was slowly phased out around the end of 1974.

*The Plus 2 shared the two-
seater's vacuum headlight
system, but its lamps were
mounted in the bonnet rather
than the wings*

CHAPTER SEVEN

Living with a Lotus

I bought my Series 2 convertible in 1971, when it was already six years old. It had had two resprays by that time—from white, to orange, to BMC Bronze Yellow—and there was evidence of some accident repair work at the rear underneath the bumper. Still, it was in fairly good condition—clean, as they say in the trade—and the engine ran smoothly, with only a faint smoke trail astern. The odometer recorded 49,735 miles, but I reckoned that this was unlikely to be the whole truth in such a sporting machine of this vintage. In the 12 years since, I have added another 104,000 miles or so to this; for the first few years, I was doing a 70-mile round trip to and from work each day by Elan, and it is only more recently that the car has enjoyed the luxury of spending extended periods in the garage—not because of unreliability, but because my job involves road-testing a large number of new models.

As I have implied throughout the previous chapters, my Elan has experienced its fair share of failures, some more exasperating to me than others. However, I cannot agree with those unbelievers— many of whom have never as much as sat in an Elan—who say you're lucky if you complete one journey without a breakdown, let alone get through a week. Elan owners tend to deprecate their cars among themselves, but they are also fiercely protective should an outsider add any serious criticism.

There are some things which defy all attempts at a cure, and one of these is the faulty door weather-sealing. I have experimented with all sorts of ingenious schemes to keep the rain out, but so far without success. If only S3 doors would fit S2 holes, I would surely be laughing; but then perhaps that would be cheating.

Shortly after I bought the car, it suffered the first of a spate of exhaust valve failures, but I eventually came to the conclusion that the trouble had been started by neglected valve clearances tightening up. Once all the valves had been changed and the clearances put right, everything was fine . . . until the head gasket blew, that is. In places there is very little between the cylinders and the waterways, and after the first gasket change, one of these areas would burn regularly. No matter how carefully I tightened the head down, the gasket would not last, so I was forced to have the head skimmed, which turned out to be the answer.

The twin-cam engine likes its diet of oil and will always use a noticeable amount. If the consumption rises, it is not necessarily due to excessive wear in the piston rings or cylinder bores. I have discovered that changing the valve guides (and the valves) can put matters to rights, so it is worth making a compression check before spending a fortune on a rebore. My engine's had its share of those, but usually because something else has gone wrong, such as a broken ring or a holed piston.

My worst engine failure came about when one of the big end bolts chose to undo itself (tab washer and all) at high speed. The result was that the rod flailed around and knocked a big groove in the side of its cylinder, before bending out of the crank-shaft's reach. This meant a new short engine, which comes without a sump, so I had to set about brazing up two neat holes punched through the old one by the errant con-rod.

Rotoflex drive shaft couplings need to be replaced regularly if dire consequences are to be avoided. This is the tougher 'Sprint' type, with metal inserts in the rubber

It is hard work trying to make the twin-cam oil-tight. There are various traditional leakage areas, such as around the cam box and the timing case, but no amount of Hermetite seems to have much effect. However, Lotus do sell a special, and very expensive, compound which is supposed to do the trick, but I'm still trying to raise the mortgage on a tube. I've already mentioned the weak water pump arrangement. All that can be done to alleviate the problem is to keep the fan belt loose and the fingers crossed.

The gearbox and final drive are reliable enough, being standard Ford parts. I have rebuilt both on my car, but only because the synchro was suffering from old age and both units were off the car anyway. This was when I did the major rebuild, brought on by rot in the chassis. Purely by chance, I had discovered that the rear towers had rotted through and although I was able to effect a temporary repair *in situ* it was obvious that the body would have to come off before long.

The bodyshell is bolted to the frame, which can be assembled into a rolling chassis before the body is dropped on

Removal turned out to be straightforward, although a crane would have been handy for lifting the heavy body off. Even hoisting one end at a time nearly pulled the garage roof down. In any event, it was just as well that I had decided to take drastic action, because it soon became clear that there was much more corrosion on the chassis than I had realised. It's amazing how quickly you can learn to make a passable weld if you are desperate. Armed

Not on the way to the junk yard, this Plus 2, but in the process of undergoing restoration

with some sheet steel of the correct thickness and an arc welder borrowed from the local hire shop, I patched holes around the towers at both ends and then primed and undersealed the whole frame. The only snag that I eventually discovered was that there was now a leak in the cross-member/vacuum reservoir, but a liberal dose of underseal cured this.

I had stripped the chassis bare to repair it, so I cleaned up all the suspension components and so on, fitted new rubber or Metalastic bushes where applicable, and renewed the brake hoses. At the same time I rebuilt the engine, as well as the diff and

gearbox. After all this, I ended up with a car whose chassis looked better than its body.

On the whole, the suspension has not been troublesome. I've changed the rear dampers a couple of times—and fortunately you can buy new inserts to screw into the struts. Having originally made the change the hard way, heating the uprights to insert complete new struts, it seemed like manna from heaven to use the inserts; but even this is fiddly, because each suspension unit is heavy and, even using spring compressors, nothing fits readily into place.

A selection of the special and standard Elan parts made by Kelvedon Motors

121

I change the lower trunnion bushes, at the front, as a matter of course before each MoT test, as these nylon Triumph parts wear quite quickly, and it is a good idea to make sure that the steering swivels are *oiled*, not greased, regularly.

My biggest suspension failure occurred when one tube of a rear A-frame broke. Fortunately, I was almost stationary in a pub car park when this happened, so no damage was done, and a judiciously applied wire coat hanger got me slowly home, where

A very special galvanized Elan chassis, with wishbone, rather than strut, rear suspension

a little brazing made a more permanent cure. Rather more dangerous, however, was the front wishbone failure which befell my brother's S3. He was lucky not to have a serious accident when the wheel folded into the wheel arch. So to any owners reading this, I counsel occasional checks of the wishbones to make sure that the bolt holes have not become elongated.

The only other real scare I have had in the car as a result of mechanical, as opposed to driver, failure, has been when a wheel, fitted by a tyre retailer, decided to come loose. I was able to stop without too much drama, to discover that the wheel—a rear one—had not been located over the drive pegs before the nut was knocked on. Not only had the wheel come loose fairly quickly, but I had lost most of the pegs, and those that remained had been pressed through. A friend of mine, with a Sprint, had a similar experience with a front wheel, only in his case the pegs caught on the brake caliper and seized the wheel solid; nasty! Moral of story: watch the tyre-fitter in action.

Along with every other Elan owner, I have had a persistent problem with the brakes, in that the pistons go rusty in the calipers. All is generally fine until it comes to changing the pads. Then the pistons will not move back, and even if they can be forced they then stick in the 'on' position as soon as they are used. I have come across no permanent solution, as yet. One company used to manufacture stainless steel pistons to fit, but this was for only a brief period, so we are back to the chrome-plated, rust-prone items.

Rear wheel bearings are a weak point, especially on the earlier cars such as mine. At some time towards the end of the S3's run the inner ones were enlarged, while the outers were changed on the S4. Unfortunately, the later bearings cannot be fitted without the new uprights, so owners like me are left

A selection of body moulds at the rear of the Lotus factory

carrying out fairly regular bearing changes. This would not be too bad if only the hubs would come off. They are fitted on tapers, and sometimes, even with the toughest extractor and the heaviest hammer, they take hours to budge.

Rotoflex couplings, especially the Sprint type, are not a problem if they are inspected regularly. Even the smallest crack warrants a change. The consequences of a failure can be horrific. I have never had one let go at high speed, but even at 30mph a flailing drive-shaft can do all sorts of damage to handbrake linkage, chassis and body. Gruesome tales are told of such disconnected shafts flying through the back of the driver's seat and causing nasty injuries.

Other troubles on my car have been fairly routine. I had a lot of clutch problems early on, these I traced to a thrust-bearing hub the first time, and a broken spring retainer in the clutch cover the second. The starter problems go on, the headlamps sag from time to time as the vacuum units rust through, and the fuel tank has to be repatched as the rust spreads (stainless ones can be had, but they are not cheap and I'm mean).

Fitting electronic ignition obliged me to swap the electrical system to negative earth (standard on

A new Elan Sprint/S4 body destined to spruce up an ageing machine somewhere

later cars): this turned out to be easier than I had expected. The radio had a change-over switch inside it, the dynamo was easy to repolarize, and the rev-counter was the only gauge which required some internal connections to be reversed. Even the battery terminals did not have to be changed, because they are of the flat type.

I've done my share of body repairs. After the blind Frenchman had finished with the car's prow, I had to fit a new half-front, which joins about halfway along the wheel arches. This proved to be rather easier than the temporary repair which I had effected by screwing all the myriad bits back together with metal straps. Once the old fibreglass had been suitably cut away, the new section could be fixed on (in this case the piece was located by four body mountings, which simplified alignment). Matting and resin applied to front and back made the joint, and a little filler, with a respray completed the job. In fact fitting new body sections—and I have done more on other Elans—is a chore which is considerably preferable to attempts to eliminate surface crazing. There is no short cut here. The fibreglass must be ground right back through its original gel-coat, and a new surface built up, using matting or tissue and new resin, topped off with a skim coat of filler. Even then there is no guarantee of a permanent cure. Flexing in the panels can soon restore the problems.

Having stopped at that, my car will probably now present me with a new set of headaches straight away, but there is nothing like a new challenge to keep the interest alive—and it's time I polished the plug caps anyway.

CHAPTER EIGHT

Elan revisited

One of the remarkable features about the Elan is that 10 years after its demise there is such a healthy demand for spare parts that there are now several companies which have been established to ensure that a suitable supply is available. Their mail order trade is thriving, and some of them have seen fit to re-source parts which, as far as the factory is concerned, are no longer available. Perhaps even more remarkable is the fact that prices of some components have actually fallen. For instance, it is possible to buy a complete set of Rotoflex couplings from the likes of Paul Matty or Christopher Neil for the approximate price of two from an official Lotus source. It must be said that there have been some wrangles between the factory and suppliers of 'alternative' parts, but I am glad to report that this has not reduced the availability of spares, which, were it to be left to Lotus, would be poor.

Many, perhaps most, parts can still be obtained from the works, but the company effectively lacks the capacity to cope with a proper spares volume for cars which have been obsolete for so long. Perhaps the biggest snag arrives at the first hurdle. The official dealers rarely seem to have anyone who actually knows about Elans anymore—and fewer still actually carry a decent stock of suitable parts. There are exceptions, of course, some of whom, such as the Norfolk Motor Company, can and will offer advice as well as a quick delivery service.

It is worth taking care when buying from an unofficial source; occassionally they will supply components which are more than non-standard in that they do not really fit. For instance, in the past I have been sold rear strut inserts (not by any of the companies mentioned), which, although they can be adapted, are patently not designed for the job, and probably have the wrong damping characteristics to boot.

It may be something of a chicken-and-egg situation, but some of the spares specialists offer a restoration service, doing jobs small or large, from a retrim to a ground-up rebuild, with new parts wherever necessary. Engine and gearbox work may be done in house, or may be put out to one of the companies which does little else but this; for

A highly modified S3 fixed head coupé

instance, you can buy off the shelf, but exchange, a short engine or whole engine and you can have it standard or tuned, as you desire.

For a time, it was difficult to buy a new chassis through Lotus, if yours had rusted away, so one or two people started to make their own. This had a dual effect of stirring the factory into action to maintain the supply of frames—galvanized, no less—and provoking a threat of legal action for alleged copyright infringement. The response of one maker, Spyder, was to put together a spaceframe backbone to fit the Elan without copying the original. This is claimed to be even stronger than the pressed steel version, though true as it may be it is an unnecessary improvement. However, at least we are now spoilt for choice—a welcome change.

One company, Vegantune, has taken the rebuilding process a stage further than anyone else, and has produced a sort of Series 5 Elan called the Evante. At the heart of this lies the engine. To replace the Lotus twin-cam, George Robinson, founder of Vegantune, designed his own two-cam head to fit on to the Ford 1600 Kent block. This is by no means radically different from the original, retaining two valves per cylinder in hemispherical

Elans come in all shapes and sizes!

chambers, but it has ironed out the problems innate in the Lotus engine's design. For instance, belt drive to the cams leaves room for a conventional water pump, and enlarged return passages move the oil back to the sump quickly. In standard trim, the VTA (as the engine is called), which is used by Caterham Car Sales for their quickest Seven, turns out an impressive 130 bhp.

The power is fed through a five-speed ZF gearbox to the usual final drive, and constant-velocity-jointed drive-shafts turn the back wheels. Bodily, the Evante is wider than the Elan, and has no bumpers, a tail spoiler and winding windows in place of the electric units. A multitude of other minor changes distinguish the two cars, and Vegantune are at pains to point out that this is a new car, not a modified Elan. Nevertheless, it is most certainly a development of the theme and thus worthy of inclusion here.

Perhaps another chapter in the Elan story is yet to come, for Lotus have let it be widely known that a new two-plus-two is on the way. Extending their co-operation with Toyota, who now have a stake in the Norfolk company, Lotus are intending to make use of engine, running gear—and perhaps much more in the new car. All the signs are that this will represent a step back to the Elan generation: an everyday sports car, in open or closed form, at a price of under £10,000—less than any existing Lotus. Certainly, with no mass-produced sports model presently in the catalogues, the time is right for such a move.

The end of the Elan was mourned by many owners and aspiring owners, who saw no real alternative in the showrooms. There are plenty, what's more, who feel that nothing has changed to alter their view since then. Well there is a story that badges have been seen at Lotus, bearing the legend 'Elan 2' . . . .

Specifications

CHASSIS
Pressed-steel box-section backbone, with splayed ends to support engine, transmission and suspension, front cross-member doubling as headlamp vacuum reservoir

BODY
Moulded fibreglass-reinforced plastic shell, with two doors, straddling backbone and bolted to it. Convertible or fixed-head styles for two-seater, but fixed-head only for Plus 2

ENGINE
In-line, four-cylinder, water-cooled unit, with cast-iron block and aluminium-alloy head. Inclined valves, in hemispherical combustion chambers, operated by twin chain-driven overhead camshafts. Five main bearings supporting cast-iron crankshaft

Engine dimensions First 22 engines (all recalled) 80.96mm bore × 72.75mm stroke = 1498cc.

All others 82.55mm bore × 72.75mm stroke = 1558cc

Compression ratio 9.5:1 (10.3:1 big-valve engines)

Fuel system 2 Weber 40DCOE carburettors except:

2 Zenith-Stromberg 175CD carburettors (some S4s);

2 Dell'Orto DHLA40 carburettors (some Sprints).

AC mechanical fuel pump, driven by original Ford camshaft.

10-gallon fuel tank (9.25 gallons S4 and Sprint).

15-gallon fuel tank (early Plus 2).

13-gallon fuel tank (later Plus 2).

Ignition system Lucas distributor, with rev-limiting rotor arm, Lucas coil, Autolite A G32 or Champion N7Y spark plugs. Static ignition timing: Weber carburettors (Mk I engines) 12 degrees btdc; Weber carburettors (Mk II engines) 10 degrees btdc; Dell'Orto carburettors 12 degrees btdc; Zenith-Stromberg carburettors 9 degrees btdc

Maximum power 90bhp at 5500rpm (standard); 93bhp at 6000rpm (S/E); approximately 95bhp (118bhp gross) at 6250rpm (Plus 2); 126bhp at 6500rpm (Sprint and Plus 2S 130)

Maximum torque 108lbft at 4000rpm (standard and S/E); 112lbft at 4000rpm (Plus 2); 113lbft at 5500rpm (Sprint and Plus 2S 130)

SPECIFICATIONS

TRANSMISSION
Clutch 8in. single-dry-plate, diaphragm-spring unit, hydraulically operated

Gearbox Four-speed, all-synchromesh (five-speed on Plus 2S 130/5 and some of the last two-seaters)

Gear ratios Semi-close ratio—4th 1.000:1, 3rd 1.396:1, 2nd 2.009:1, 1st 2.972:1, close ratio—4th 1.000:1, 3rd 1.230:1, 2nd 1.636:1, 1st 2.510:1; five speed—5th 0.80:1, 4th 1.00:1, 3rd 1.37:1, 2nd 2.00:1, 1st 3.2:1

Final drive Chassis-mounted, hypoid-bevel unit, with open shafts, incorporating twin Rotoflex couplings, driving rear wheels

Final-drive ratio 3.90:1 (S1, S2 and early S3); 3.777:1 (later S3, S4, Sprint and Plus 2); 3.555:1 (optional on two-seater)

SUSPENSION
Front Independent by upper and lower pressed-steel wishbones, coaxial coil spring/damper units and an anti-roll bar.

Rear Independent by coil spring/damper struts and lower transverse A-frames

STEERING
Rack and pinion, with telescopic steering column. 2½ turns from lock to lock

BRAKES
Outboard discs front and rear, 9½ in. front (10 in. on Plus 2) and 10 in. rear. Servo assistance on S/E, Sprint and Plus 2. Handbrake operating on separate rear pads

WHEELS AND TYRES
4½J × 13in. steel wheels—bolt on for S2, centre-lock optional for S2 and standard thereafter; 5½J × 13in. centre-lock steel wheels for Plus 2 series. 5.20 × 13 cross-ply tyres for early S1; 145 × 13 radial-ply tyres for late S1, S2 and S3; 155 × 13 radial-ply tyres optional for S/E, standard for S4 and Sprint; 165 × 13 radial-ply tyres for Plus 2 series

ELECTRICAL EQUIPMENT
Lucas C40 dynamo (Lucas 17ACR alternator on Plus 2S); 39 ampère-hour battery; vacuum-operated pop-up headlamps; electric windows on S3, S4, Sprint and Plus 2 models

DIMENSIONS
Overall length 12ft 1in. (two-seater), 14ft 0in. (Plus 2); overall width 4ft 8in. (two-seater), 5ft 3½in. (Plus 2); height 3ft 9¼in. (S1, S2), 3ft 9½in. (S3, S4 and Sprint convertible), 3ft 10½in. S3, S4 and Sprint coupé), 3ft 11in. (Plus 2); ground clearance 6in. (two-seater), 5.6in. (Plus 2); wheelbase 7ft 0in. (two-seater), 8ft 0in. (Plus 2); front track 3ft 11in. (two-seater), 4ft 6in. (Plus 2); rear track 4ft 0½in. (S1, S2), 3ft 11in. (S3 onwards), 4ft 7in. (Plus 2); turning circle 29ft 6in. (S1, S2 and S3), 33ft 6in. (S4, Sprint), 28ft 0in. (Plus 2)

WEIGHT
1410lb (S1), 1485lb (S2), 1530lb (S3 S/E coupé, S3 convertible, S4 convertible), 1540lb (S3 S/E convertible, S4 coupé, S4 S/E and Sprint convertible), 1550lb (S4 S/E and Sprint coupé), 1880lb (Plus 2), 1970lb (Plus 2S)

PERFORMANCE
Maximum speed 115mph (3.9 final drive, std engine), 120mph (3.777 final drive, std engine), 125mph (3.555 final drive, S/E engine), 120mph (Sprint), 120mph (Plus 2). Acceleration, 0–60mph 9 sec. (standard), 8 sec. (S/E), 7 sec. (Sprint), 9 sec. (Plus 2), 7.5 sec. (Plus 2S 130)

Acknowledgements

Author Ian Ward has been living 'Lotus Elan' for too long now to warrant explicit thanks to anyone in helping him prepare this book—he simply can't remember all the people he has consulted on the subject over those long years. Apart from a general 'thank you' he has to single out one man—Donovan McLauchlan of the Lotus Group of Companies. Ever enthusiastic, ever helpful Don never fails to come up with an answer, if not the answer. His door is ever open—thanks.

Mirco Decet gathered the photographs, shooting many along the way himself. All the colour is his except for one—that came from editor Tim Parker. Mirco received generous help from a number of people, some owners of the delightful Elan. There was Mark Rolfe of the Lotus Owners Club, Sussex Sports Cars of Forest Row in Sussex, a Mr Miller of Saxmundum in Suffolk and Monitor Advertising. Finally, author Ian Ward added shots of his own to the sum.

Index

A
Ansdale, Richard **21**
Autocar **21**

B
BMC **18**
BRM **21, 59**

C
Caterham Car Sales **35, 130**
Chapman, Colin **7–11, 15, 16, 18, 21, 26, 41, 53, 56, 61, 82**
Clark, Jim **10, 20, 27, 53**
Cosworth Engineering **35, 59**

E
Earls Court Motor Show **13, 15, 38**

F
Facel Vega **22**
Ferrari **27**
Ford Motor Company **9, 16–18**
  Anglia **39, 99**
  Classic **30, 36**
  Corsair **36**
  Cortina **30**

G
Goodwood TT **26**

H
Hayes, Walter **18**

Hethel (Norfolk) **10, 12, 35, 101, 102**
Hickman, Ron **9, 14**
Hillman Imp **94**

J
Jaguar E type **15, 27**

K
Kelvedon Motors **121**
Kirwan-Taylor, Peter **8**

L
London Motor Show (1962) **15**
Lotus
  Cortina **18**
  Elite **8, 9, 11, 15–18, 21, 41, 114**
  Europa **35, 82, 110**
  Plus 2 **34, 35**

M
Matty, Paul **127**
Metier **98**
Morris Marina **92**
Mundy, Harry **21, 22, 34**

N
Neil, Christopher **127**
Norfolk Motor Company **127**
Nürburgring
  1962 **27**
  1964 **29**

P
Prestwich, J.A. **35**

R
Rigg, Diana **41**
Rindt, Jochen **90, 92**
Robinson, George **129**
Rudd, Tony **41, 92**

S
Silverstone 1964 **28**
Spyder **129**

T
Team Elite **28**
Toyota **130**
Triumph **16, 44**
  GT6 **99**
  Herald **44**
  Spitfire **44, 79**
  Vitesse **44**

V
Vauxhall **55, 82**
Vegantune **129, 130**
Evante **129**
Villiers **35**

W
Warner, Graham **26, 27**
Wolseley Hornet **99**